For Lex, Ginger, Bonny and everlasting George.

Published in 2018 by Melbournestyle Books
155 Clarendon Street, South Melbourne
Victoria 3205, Australia
www.melbournestyle.com.au

All rights reserved. No part of this publication may be reproduced, stored in a
retrieval system or transmitted in any form by any means, electronic, mechanical,
photocopying, recording or otherwise, without the prior written permission of the
publishers and copyright holders. The publishers regret any errors or omissions.

All illustrations, design & concept © Maree Coote 2018

Printed in China by C&C Offset Printing on wood-free paper

A catalogue record for this book is available from
the National Library of Australia

National Library of Australia Cataloguing-in-Publication entry:

Coote, Maree, author, illustrator.

Alphabeasts: An A to Z of alphabetical animals
/ Maree Coote, author, illustrator.

ISBN 978-0-9924917-7-2 (hbk.)

Subjects:

1. Graphic design (Typography) — Juvenile literature.
2. Visual poetry, Australian — Pictorial works — Juvenile literature.
3. Graphic design (Typography) — Pictorial works — Juvenile literature.
4. English language — Alphabet — Pictorial works — Juvenile literature.
5. Alphabet in art — Pictorial works — Juvenile literature.
6. Animals — Pictorial works — Juvenile literature.

10 9 8 7 6 5 4 3 2 1

MELBOURNESTYLE
BOOKS
www.melbournestyle.com.au

www.cleverkids.net.au

ALPHABEASTS

An A to Z of alphabetical animals

LOOK-AND-FIND • EVERY PICTURE MADE WITH THE LETTERS OF ITS OWN NAME.

LETTER ART

The way I look
is part genetic
But it's also
alphabetic.
Look and find each
letter shape
To spell a very
handsome ape.

Sometimes
letters may repeat
To make more eyes
or hair or feet,
But back-to-front
or upside-down,
Every letter
can be found!

MAREE COOTE

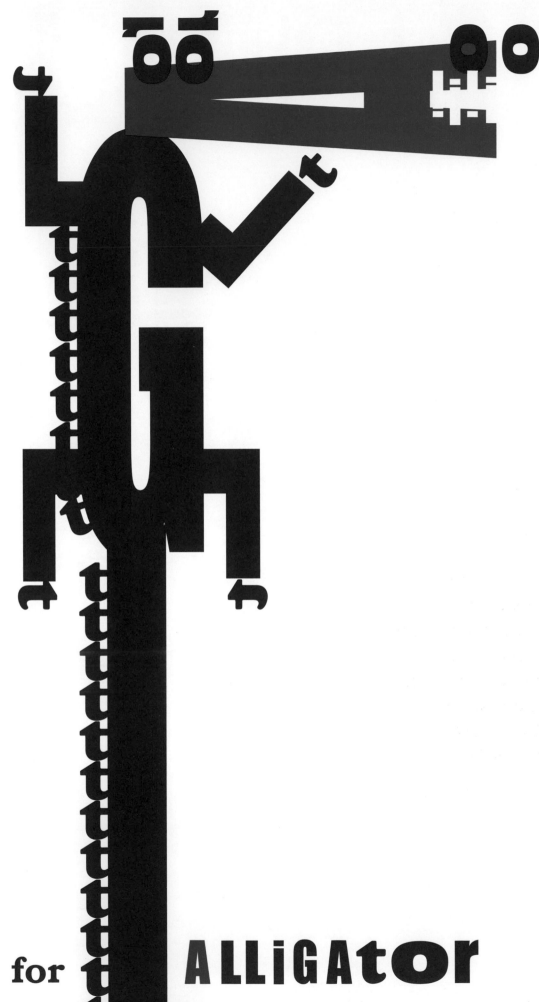

A is for ALLiGAtor

B is for Bug

C is for Camel

D is for DRAGON

e is for elephant

f is for flAMiNGO

G is for GOrilla

H is for HiPPOPOtAMUS

J is for JAGUAR

K is for KoaLa

L is for Lion

M is for MOUSE

N is for NUMbAt

is for OWL

P is for PIGEON

Q is for QUOKKA

R is for ROOStER

t is for tORtOiSE

V is for VULTURE

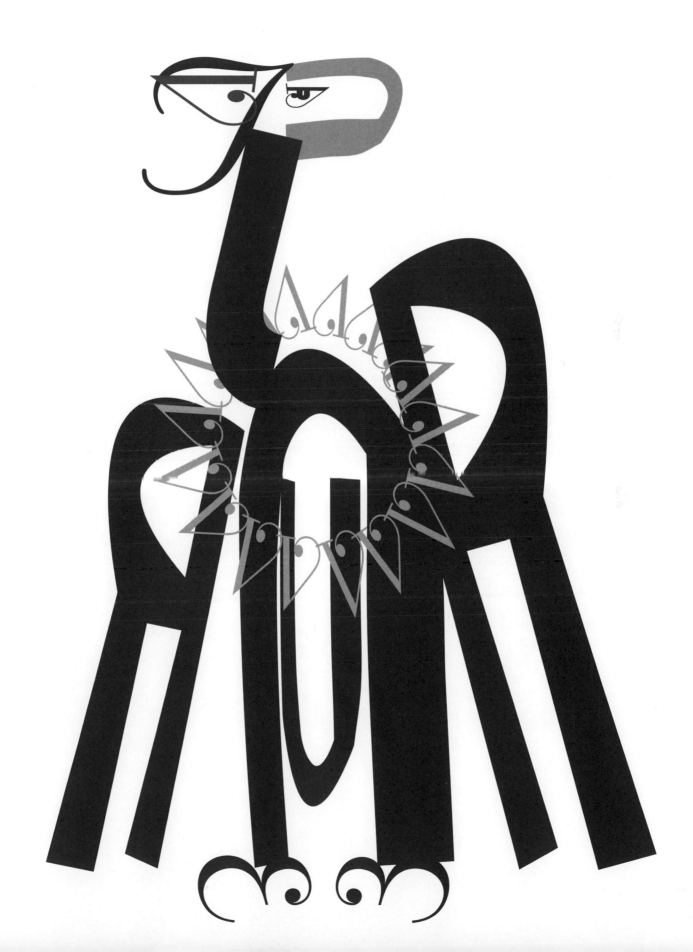

W is for WOMBAT

X is for XRAY FISH

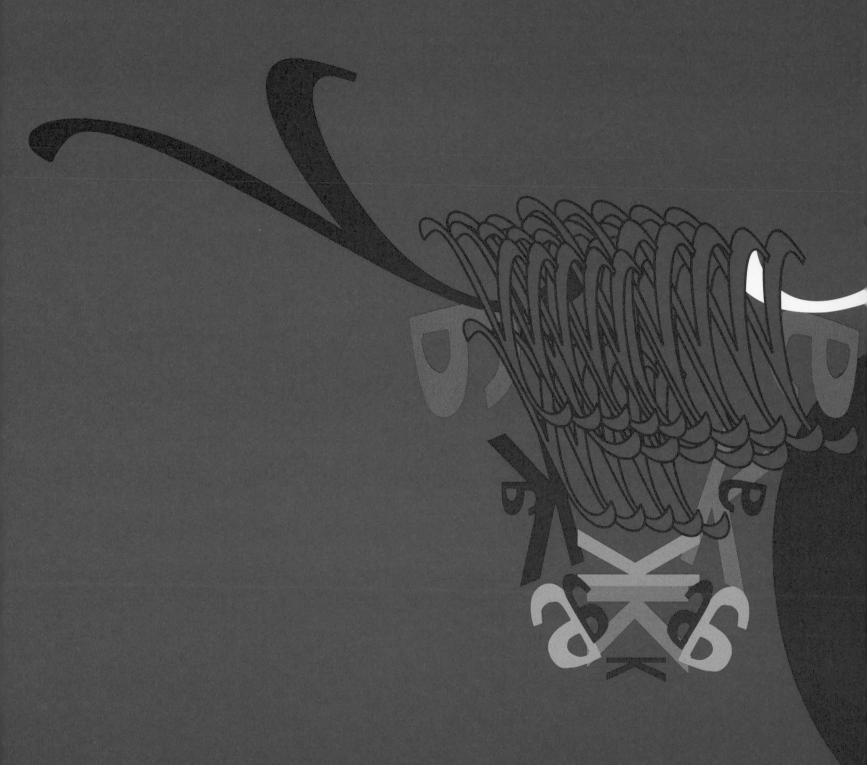

y is for yak

Jaguar